# Famous & Fun Deluxe Collec

### 23 Pieces from Famous & Fun:
### Pop, Classics, Favorites, Rock, Duets
# Carol Matz

*Famous & Fun Deluxe Collection, Book 4*, contains 23 well-loved selections drawn from the following books:

- Famous & Fun Pop, Book 4
- Famous & Fun Favorites, Book 4
- Famous & Fun Duets, Book 4
- Famous & Fun Classics, Book 4
- Famous & Fun Rock, Book 4
- Famous & Fun Pop Duets, Book 4

These teacher-tested arrangements are student favorites, and can be used as a supplement to any method. In addition to the wide variety of styles featured in this collection, a few equal-part (primo/secondo) duets are also included for students to have fun with ensemble playing.

**Alfred**

Produced by
Alfred Music
P.O. Box 10003
Van Nuys, CA 91410-0003
alfred.com

Prouced in USA.

ISBN-10: 1-4706-1106-6
ISBN-13: 978-1-4706-1106-4

# (Meet) The Flintstones

Words and Music by Joseph Barbera,
William Hanna and Hoyt Curtin
Arranged by Carol Matz

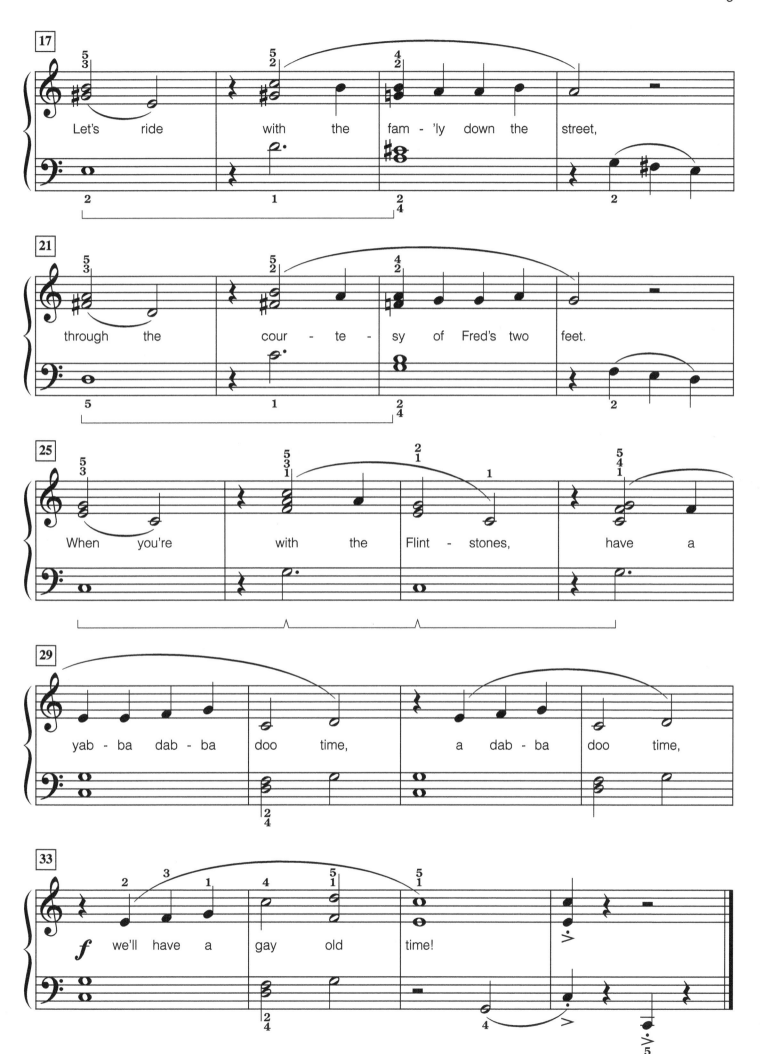

# James Bond Theme

By Monty Norman
Arranged by Carol Matz

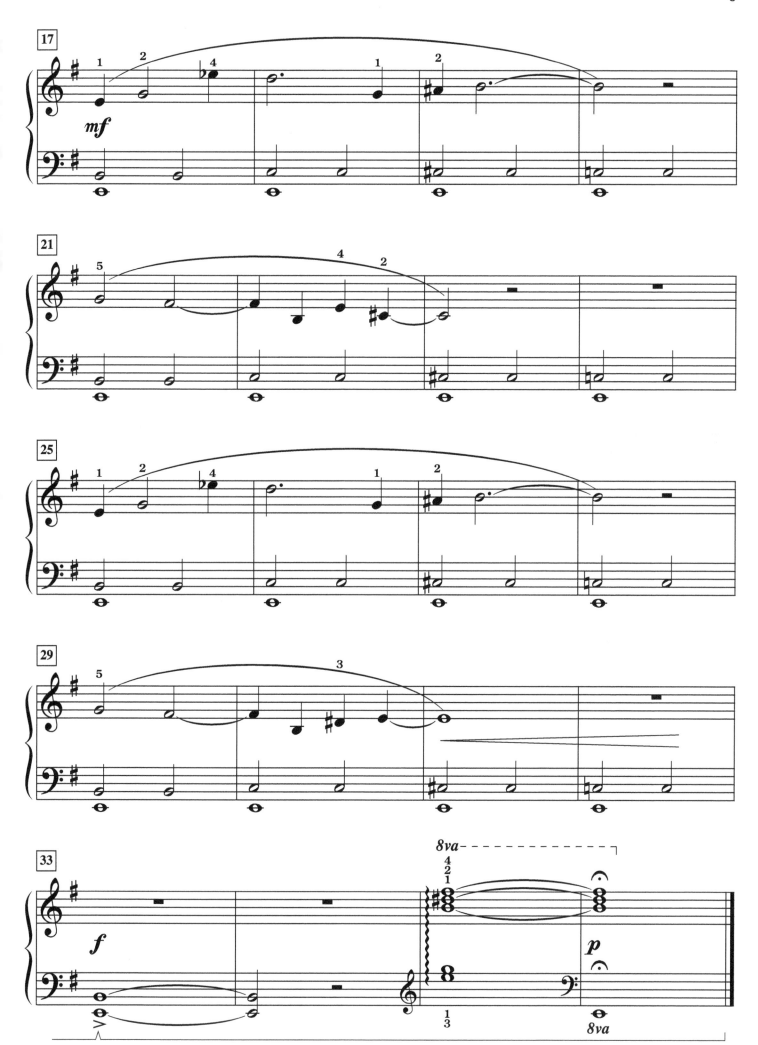

# Wipe Out

By The Surfaris
Arranged by Carol Matz

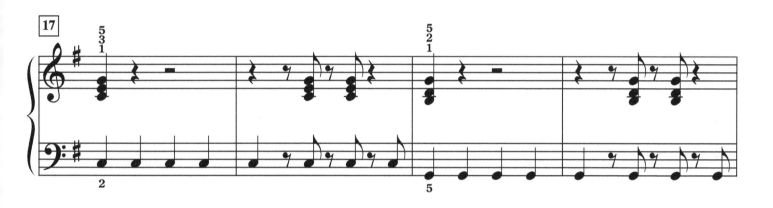

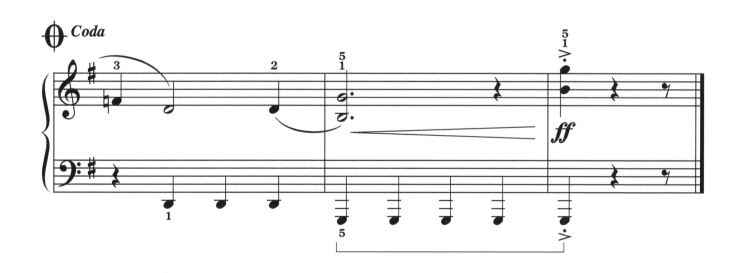

# Can You Feel the Love Tonight?

(from Walt Disney's *The Lion King*)

Music by Elton John
Words by Tim Rice
Arranged by Carol Matz

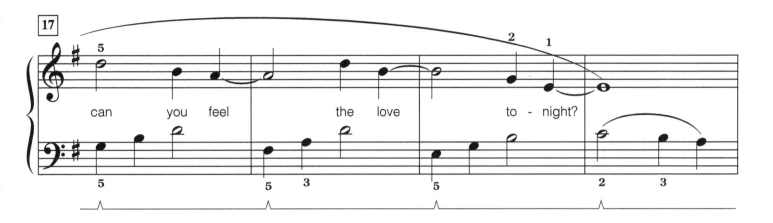

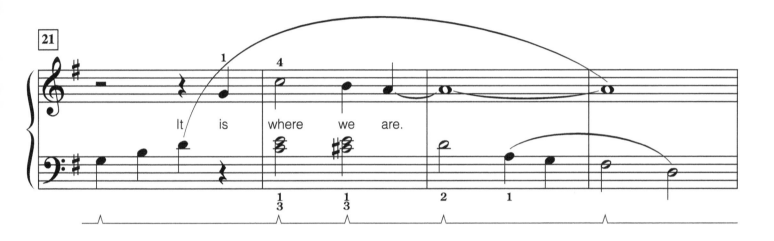

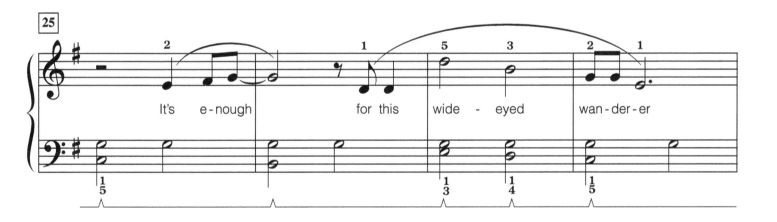

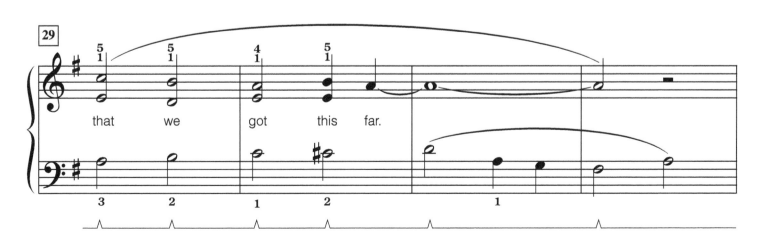

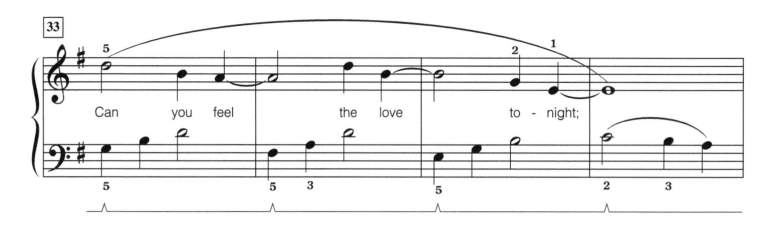

Can you feel the love to - night;

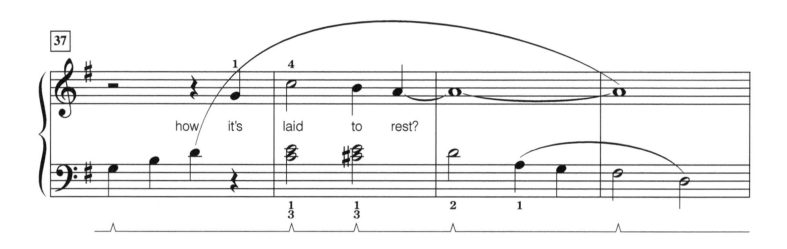

how it's laid to rest?

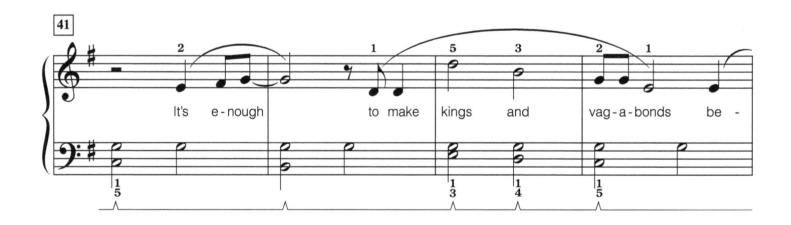

It's e - nough to make kings and vag - a - bonds be -

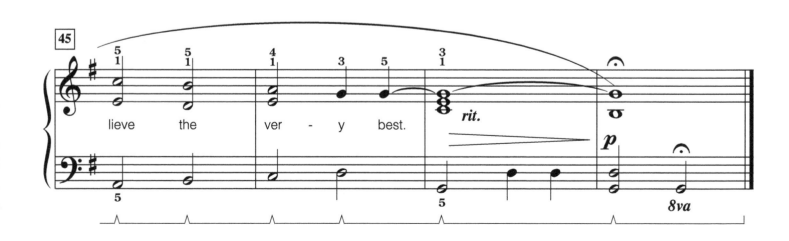

lieve the ver - y best. *rit.* *p*

*8va*

# Star Wars®

## (Main Title)

Music by **JOHN WILLIAMS**
Arranged by Carol Matz

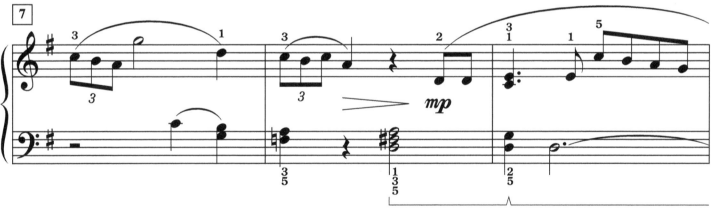

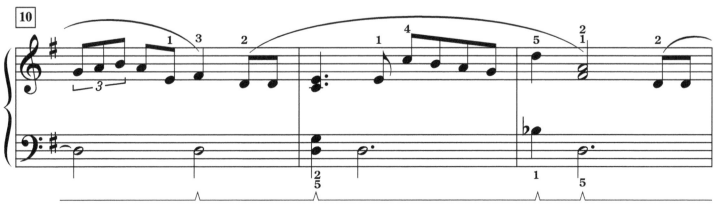

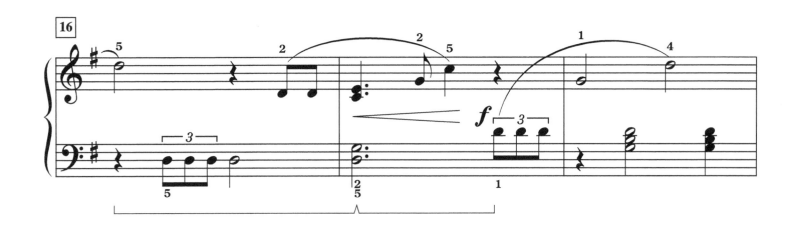

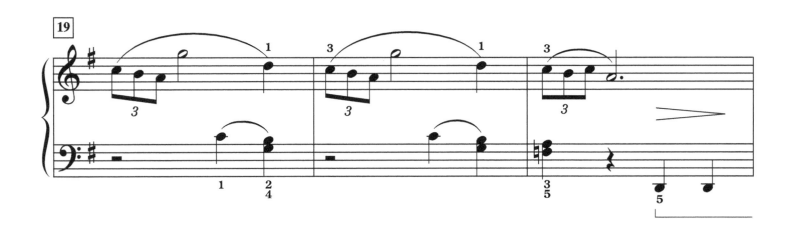

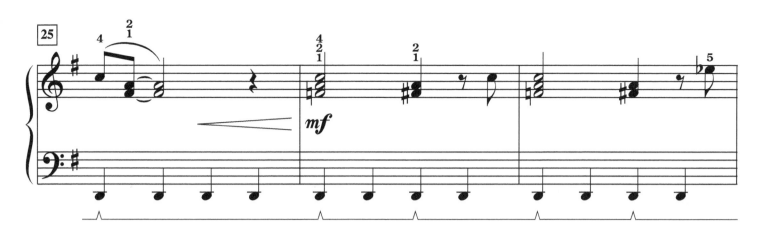

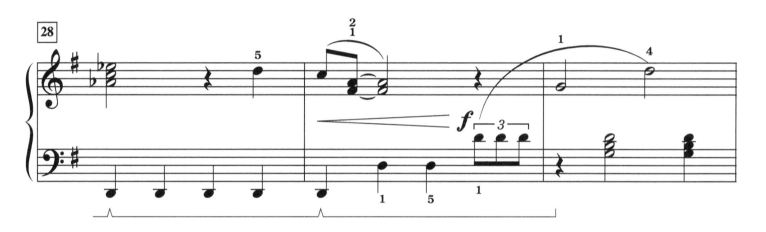

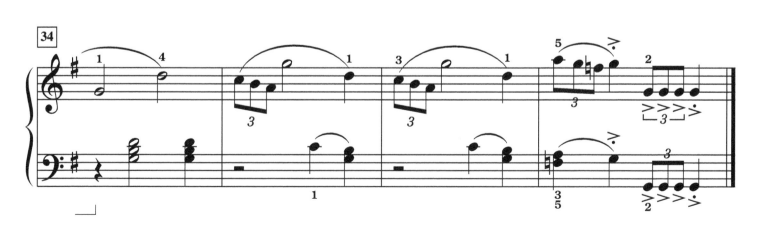

# Waltz

(Op. 39, No. 15)

Johannes Brahms (1833–1897)
Arranged by Carol Matz

**Tenderly**

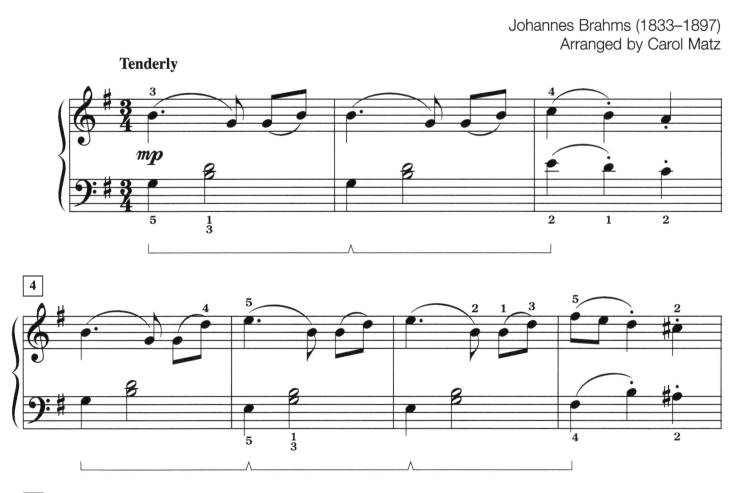

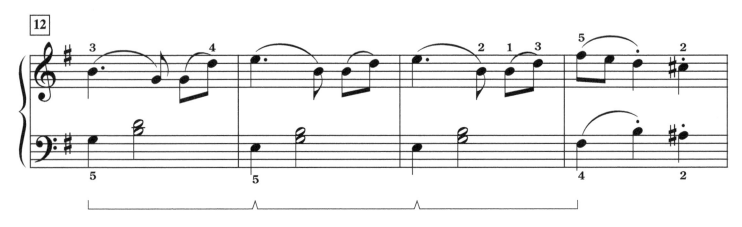

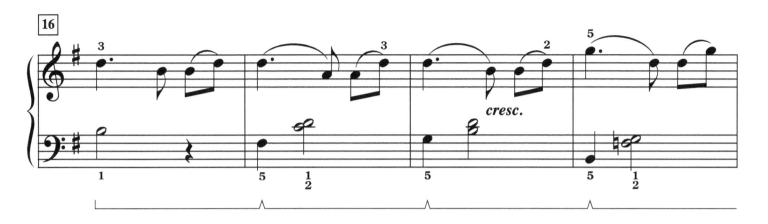

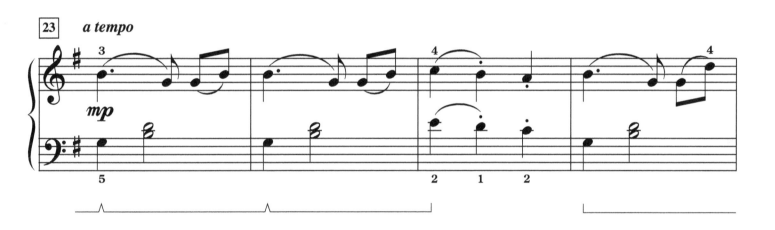

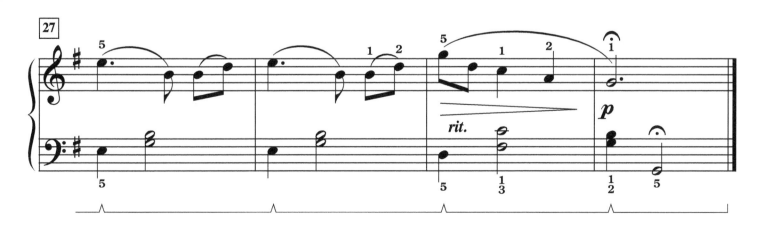

# Hungarian Dance

## (No. 5)

Johannes Brahms (1833–1897)
Arranged by Carol Matz

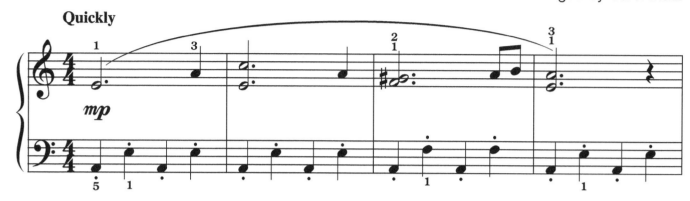

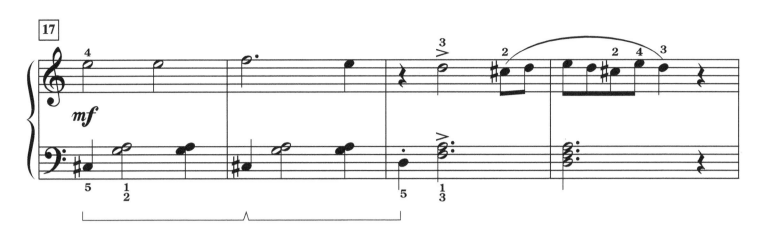

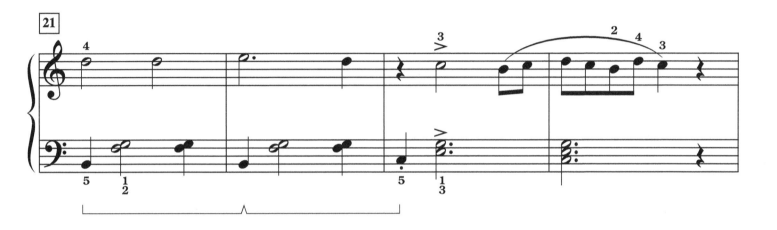

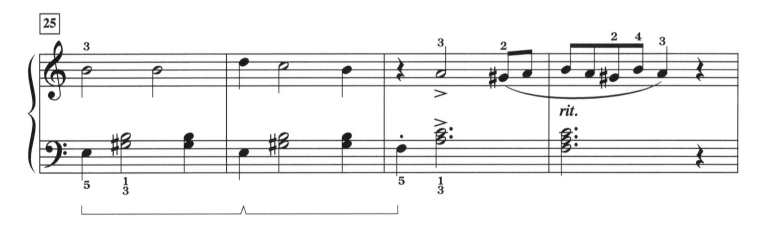

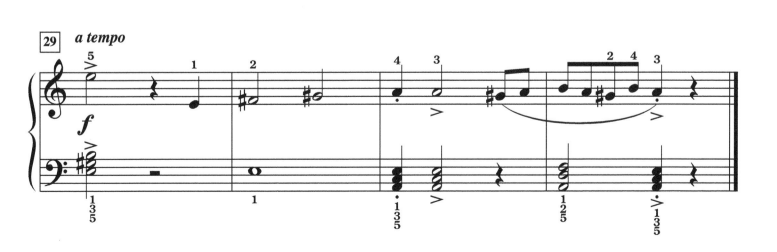

# Overture to
# The Barber of Seville

Gioachino Rossini (1792–1868)
Arranged by Carol Matz

# Eine Kleine Nachtmusik
## (A Little Night Music)
(First Movement)

Wolfgang Amadeus Mozart (1756–1791)
Arranged by Carol Matz

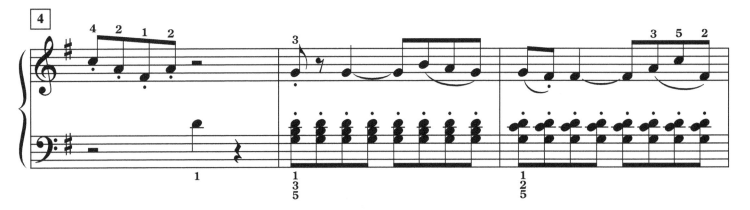

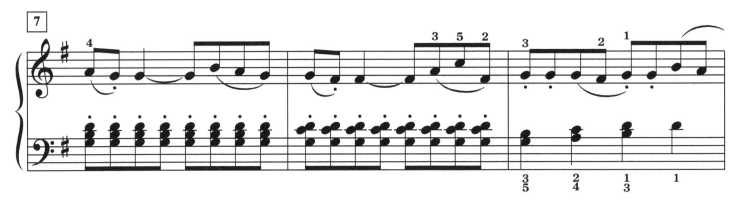

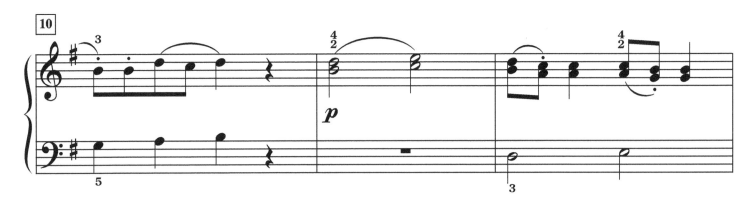

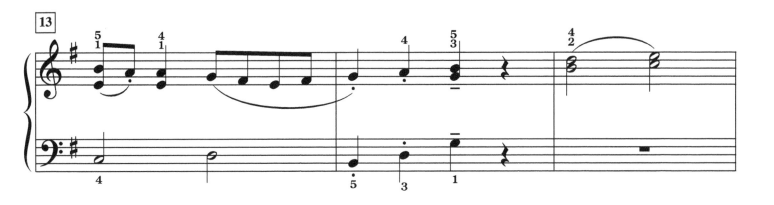

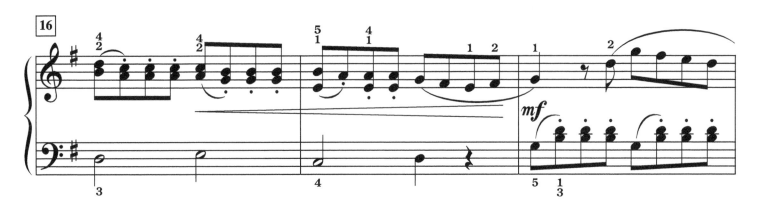

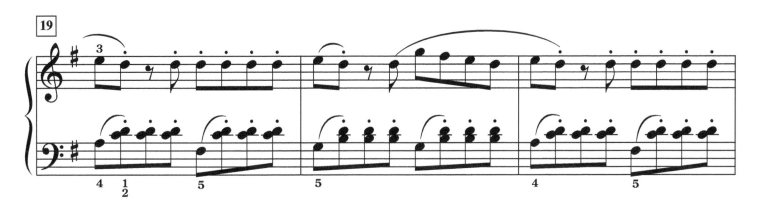

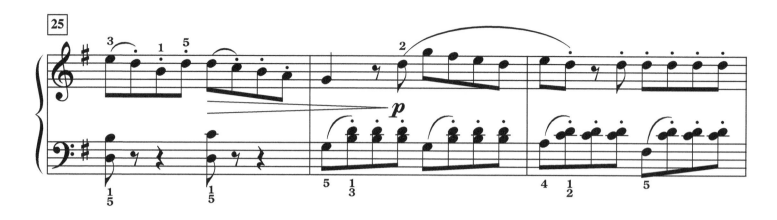

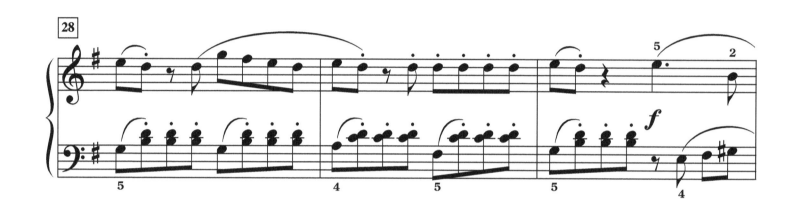

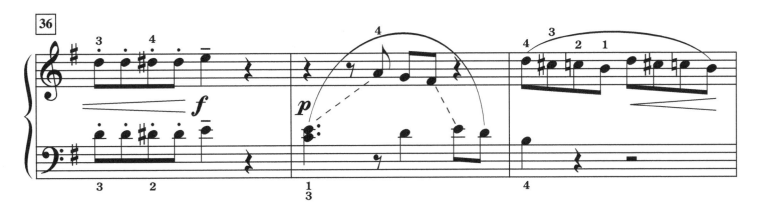

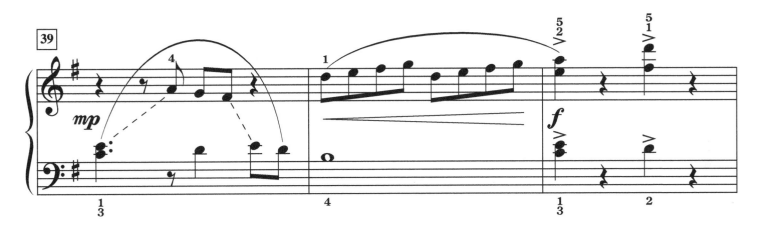

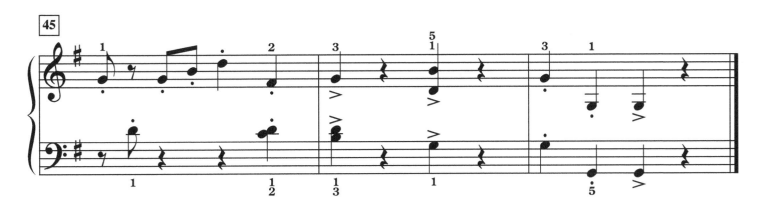

# The Entertainer

Scott Joplin
Arranged by Carol Matz

# Greensleeves

Traditional English
Arranged by Carol Matz

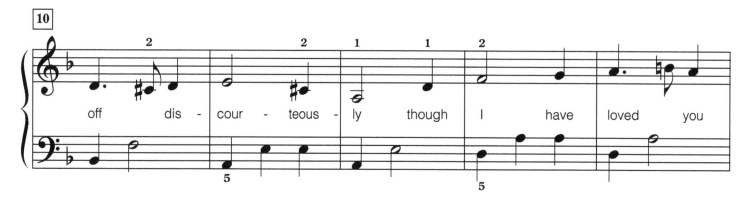

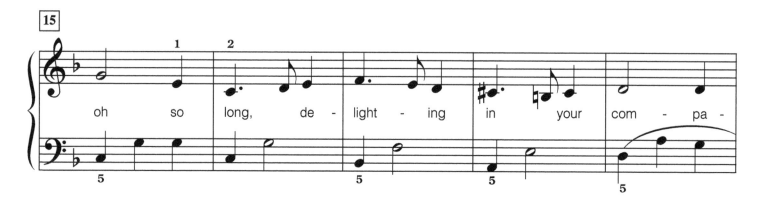

# America the Beautiful

Words by Katherine Lee Bates
Music by Samuel A. Ward
Arranged by Carol Matz

# Irish Washerwoman

Traditional Irish
Arranged by Carol Matz

# Wedding Tarantella

Traditional Italian Dance
Arranged by Carol Matz

# (We're Gonna) Rock Around the Clock

Words and Music by
Max C. Freedman and Jimmy De Knight
Arranged by Carol Matz

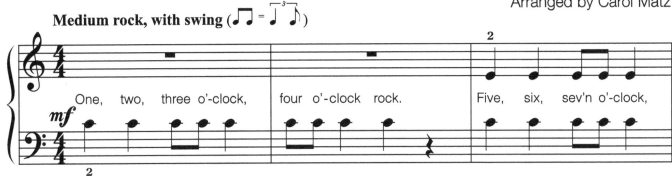

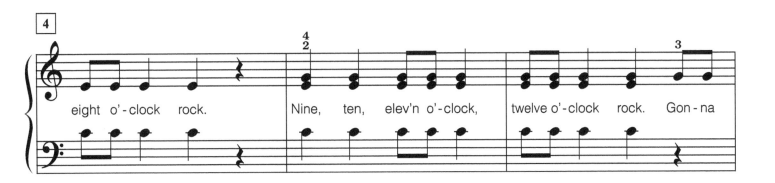

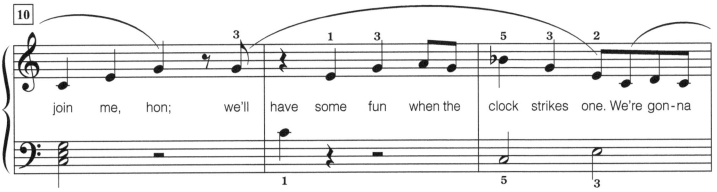

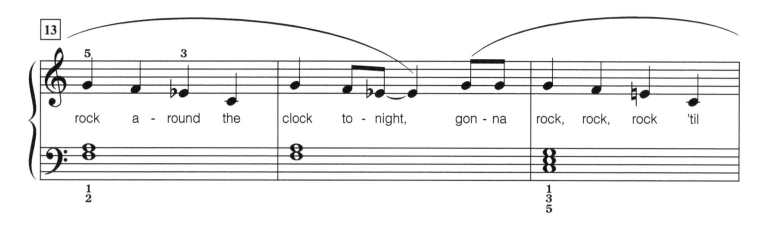

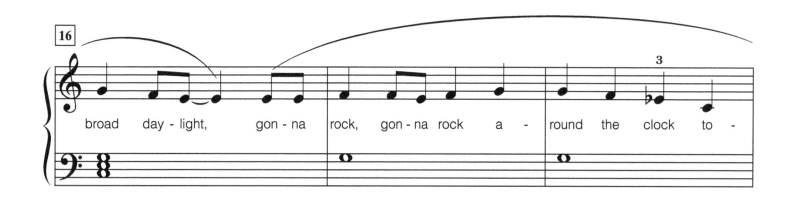

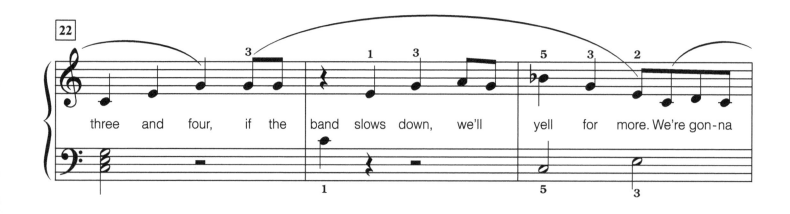

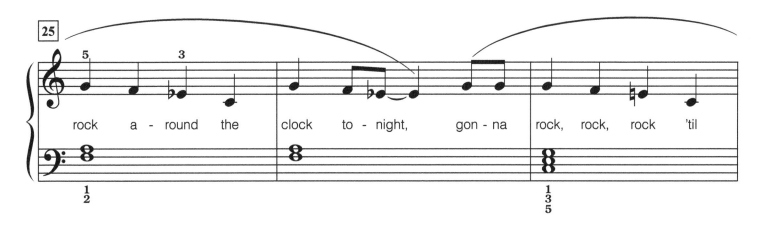

rock a - round the clock to - night, gon - na rock, rock, rock 'til

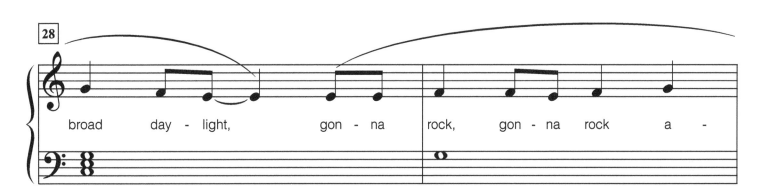

broad day - light, gon - na rock, gon - na rock a -

round the clock to - night!

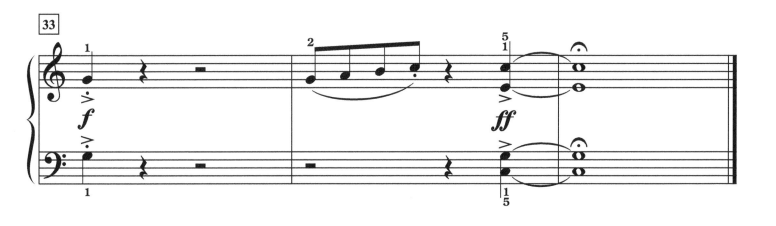

# Great Balls of Fire

Words and Music by
Otis Blackwell and Jack Hammer
Arranged by Carol Matz

**Fast rock**

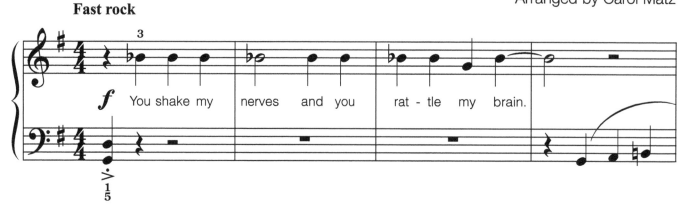

You shake my nerves and you rat - tle my brain.

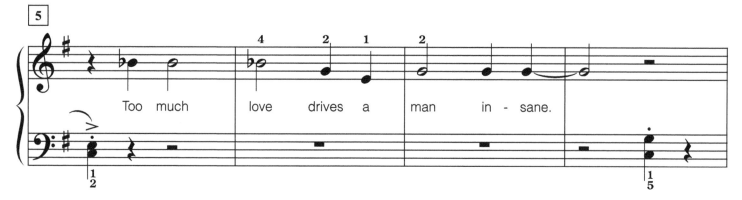

Too much love drives a man in - sane.

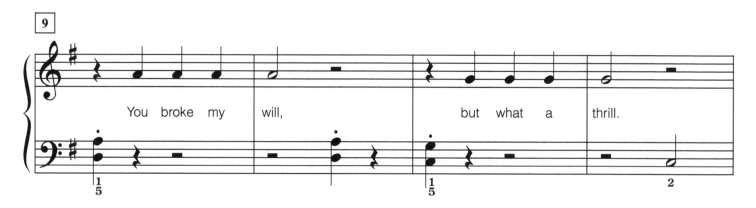

You broke my will, but what a thrill.

Good - ness gra - cious, great balls of fire!

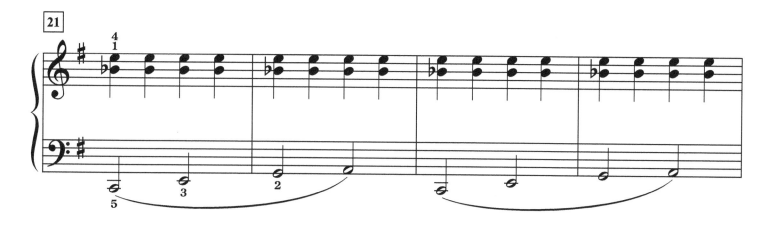

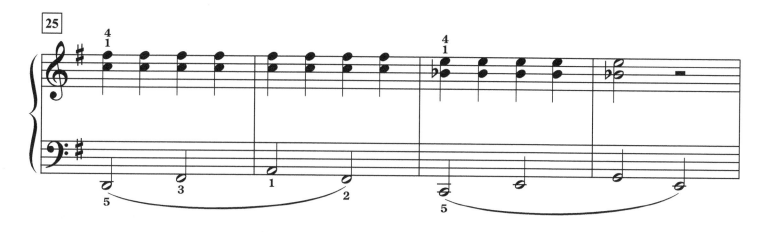

Good - ness gra - cious, great balls of fire!

# It's My Party

Words and Music by Herb Wiener,
John Gluck and Wally Gold
Arranged by Carol Matz

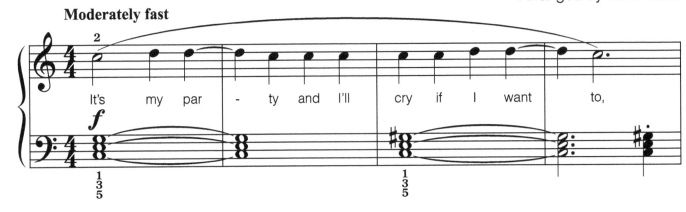

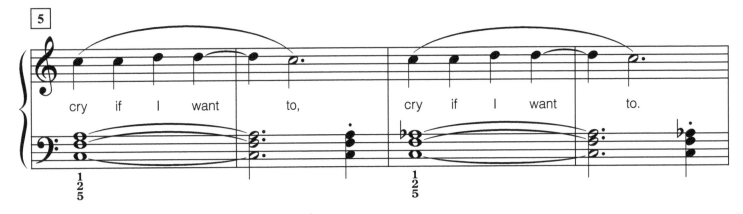

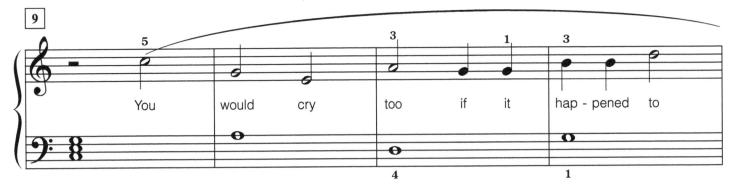

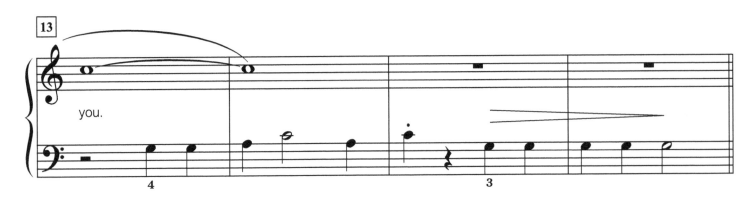

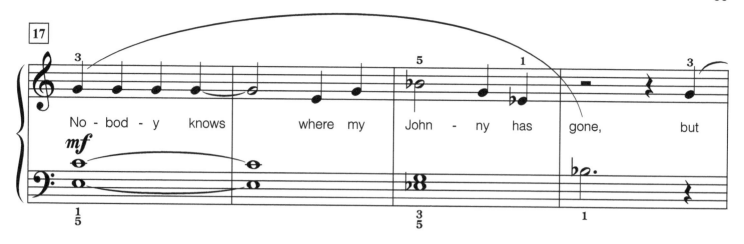

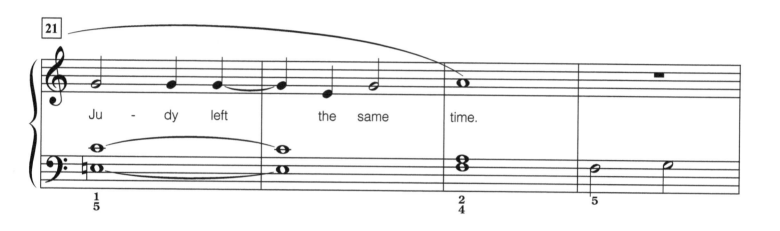

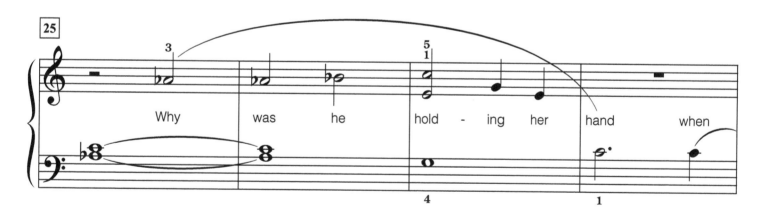

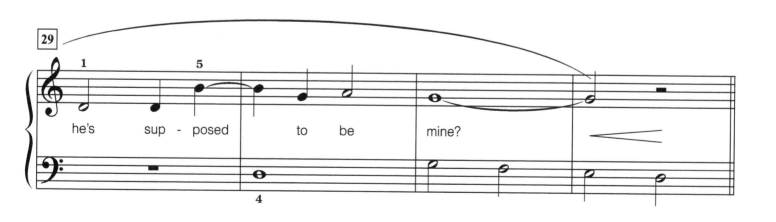

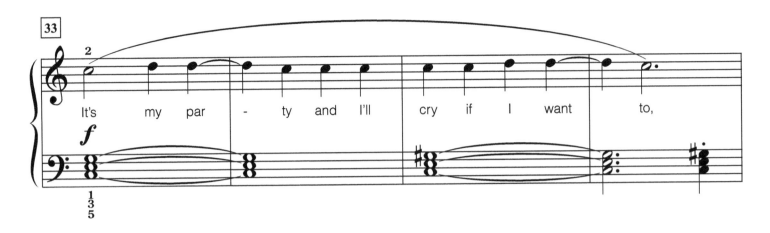

It's my par - ty and I'll cry if I want to,

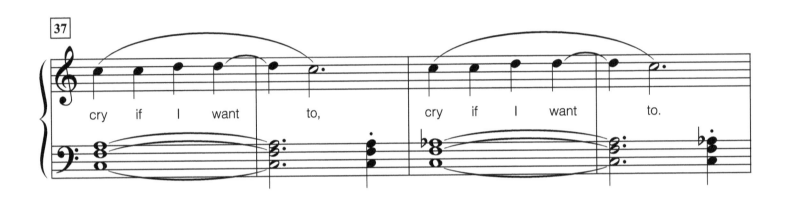

cry if I want to, cry if I want to.

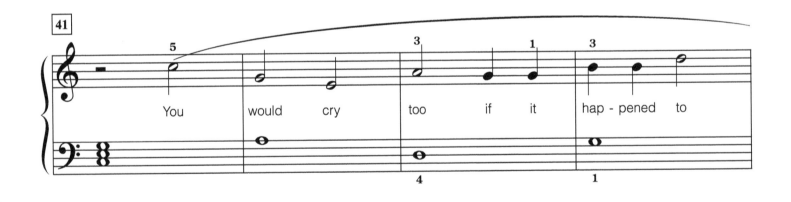

You would cry too if it hap - pened to

you.

# Boulevard of Broken Dreams

Words by Billie Joe
Music by Green Day
Arranged by Carol Matz

42

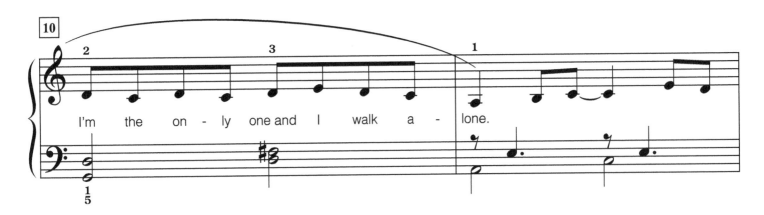

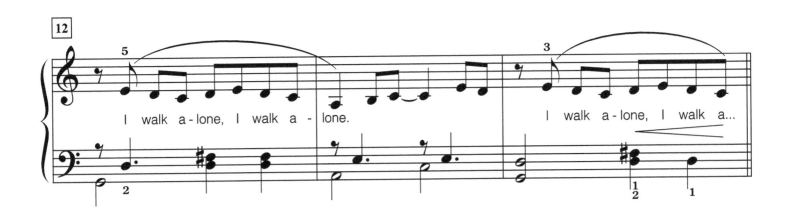

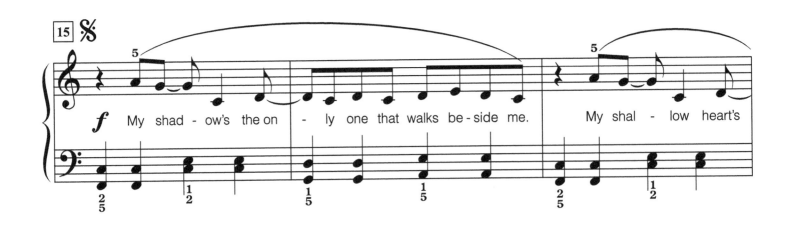

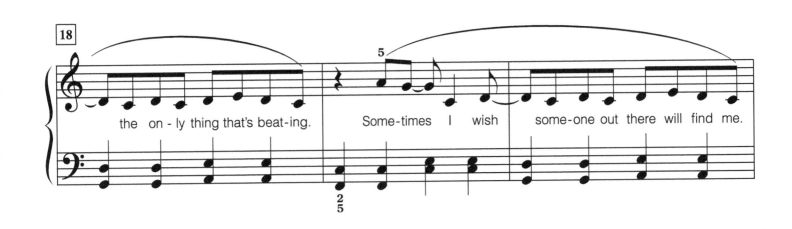

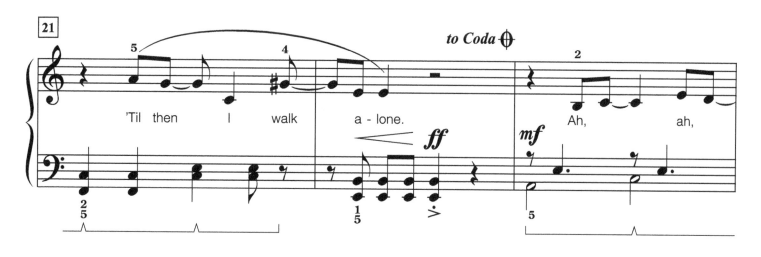

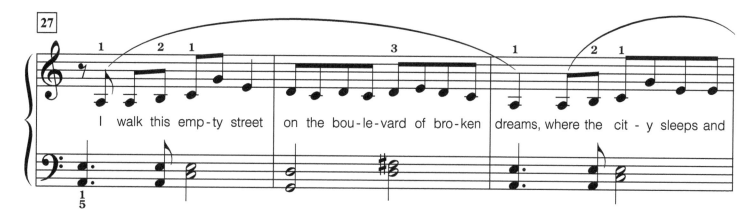

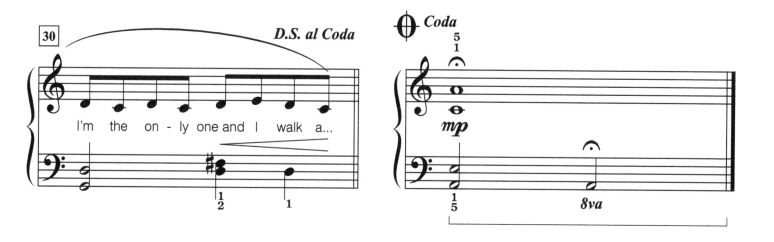

# Hey There Delilah

Words and Music by Tom Higgenson
Arranged by Carol Matz

45

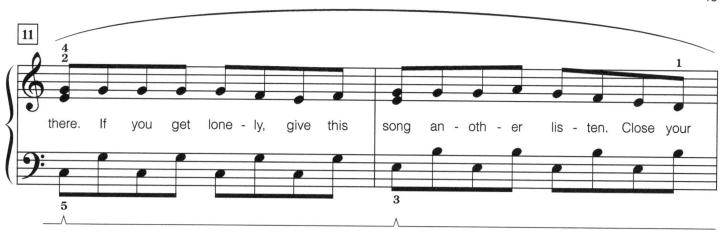

there. If you get lone - ly, give this song an - oth - er lis - ten. Close your

eyes. Listen to my voice, it's my dis - guise. I'm by your

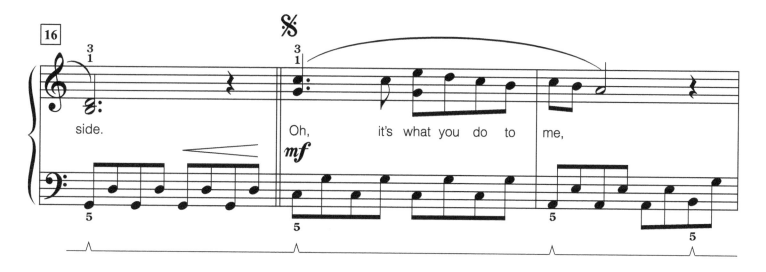

side. Oh, it's what you do to me,

oh, it's what you do to me. Oh, it's what you do to

know that none of them have felt this way. De - li -lah, I can pro-mise you that

by the time that we get through, the world will nev - er, ev - er be the

D.S. al Coda

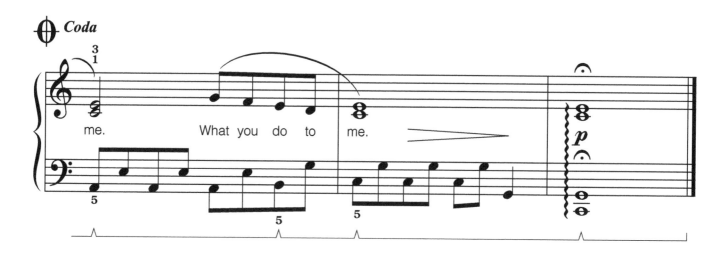

same, and you're to blame.

Coda

me. What you do to me.

# Chim Chim Cher-ee

(from Walt Disney's *Mary Poppins*)

**Secondo**

Words and Music by
Richard M. Sherman and Robert B. Sherman
Arranged by Carol Matz

# Chim Chim Cher-ee

(from Walt Disney's *Mary Poppins*)

**Primo**

Words and Music by
Richard M. Sherman and Robert B. Sherman
Arranged by Carol Matz

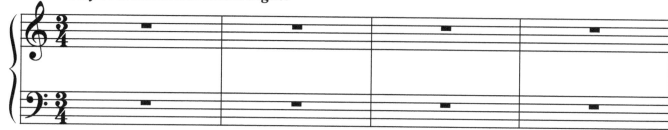

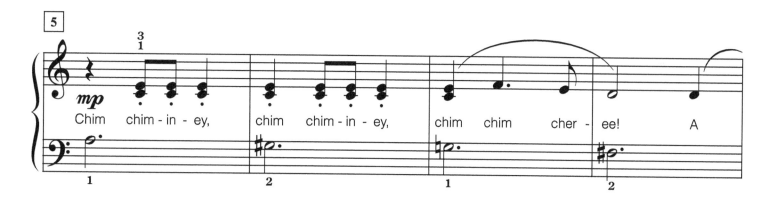

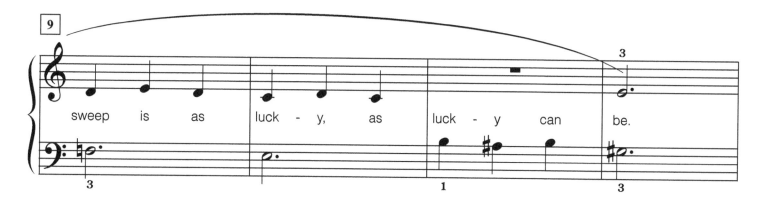

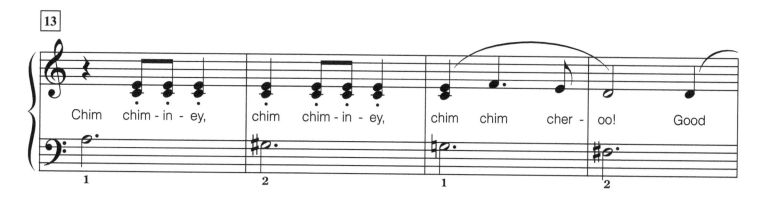

## Secondo

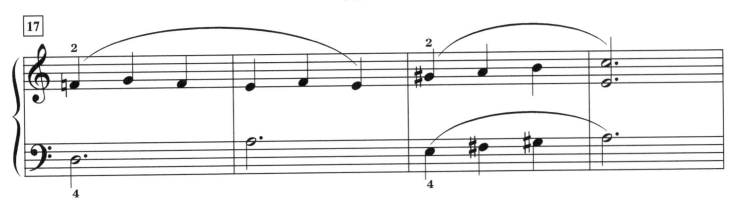

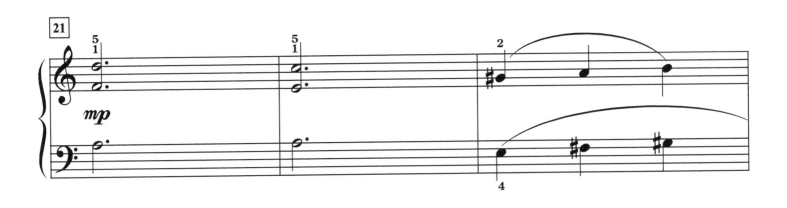

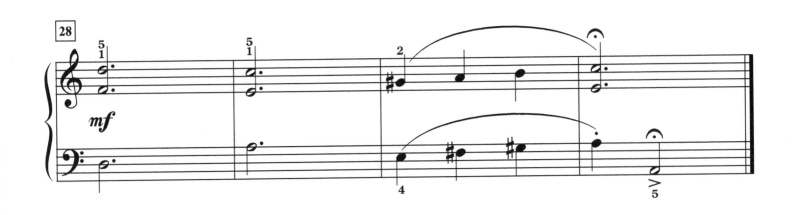

**Primo**

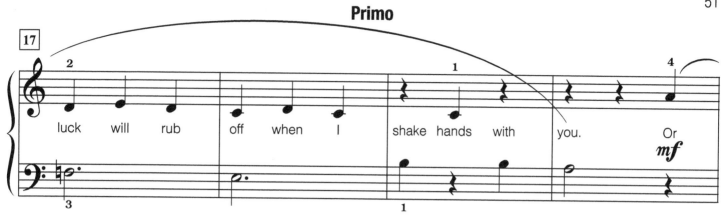

luck will rub off when I shake hands with you. Or

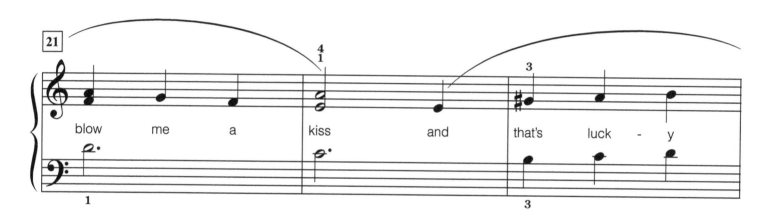

blow me a kiss and that's luck - y

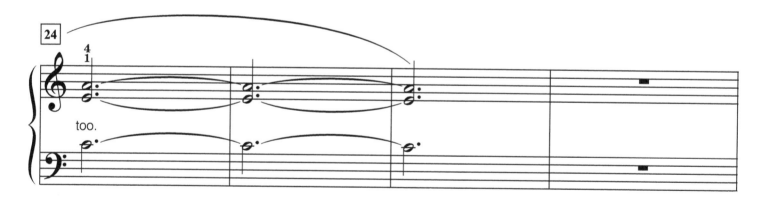

too.

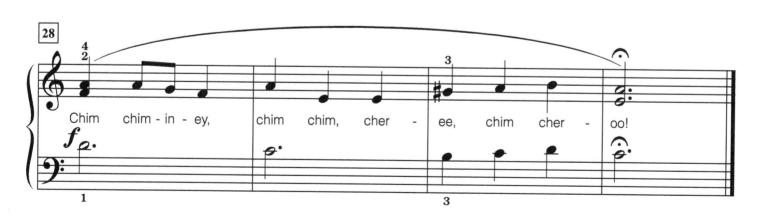

Chim chim - in - ey, chim chim, cher - ee, chim cher - oo!

# Skaters Waltz

## Secondo

Emil Waldteufel
Arranged by Carol Matz

# Skaters Waltz

## Primo

Emil Waldteufel
Arranged by Carol Matz

**Moderately**

*Play both hands one octave higher*

## Secondo

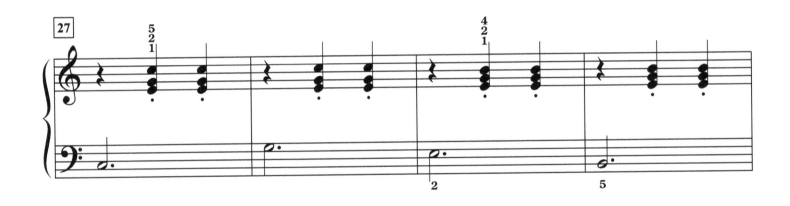

*D.C. al Fine*

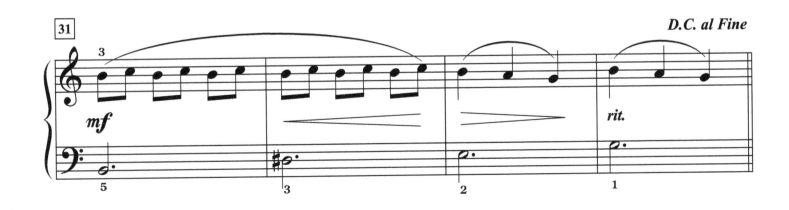

**Primo**

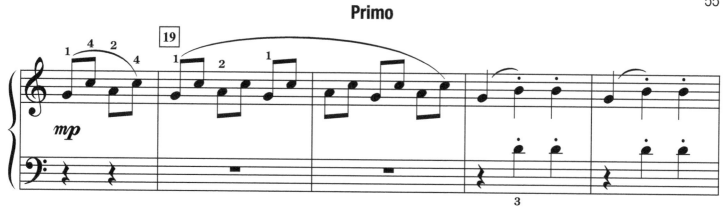

*D.C. al Fine*

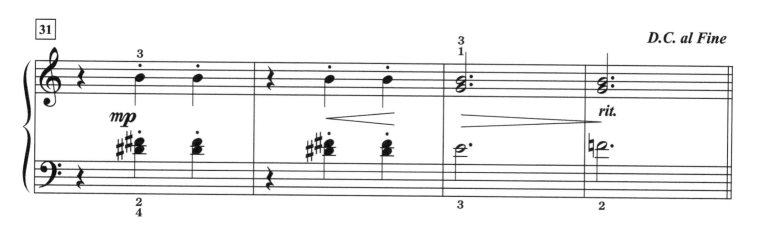

# Polovetsian Dance

## Secondo

Alexander Borodin
Arranged by Carol Matz

# Polovetsian Dance

## Primo

Alexander Borodin
Arranged by Carol Matz

**Flowing**

*Play both hands one octave higher*

**Secondo**

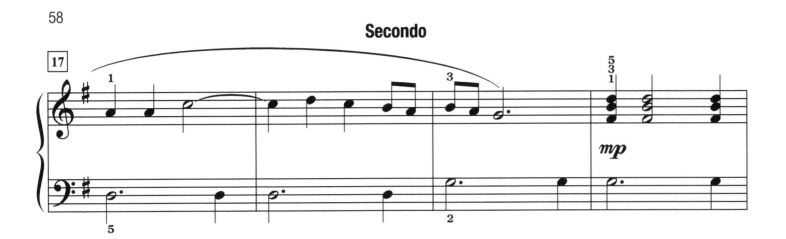

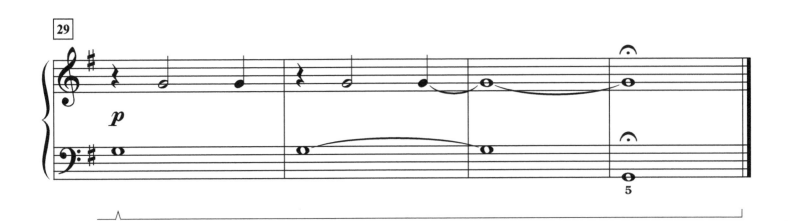

## Primo

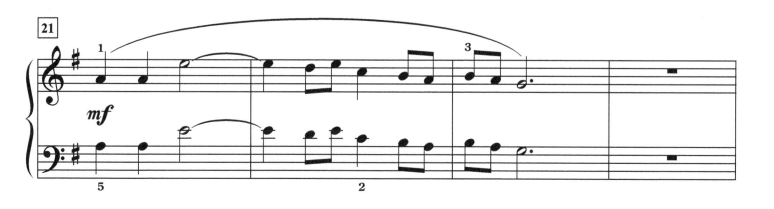

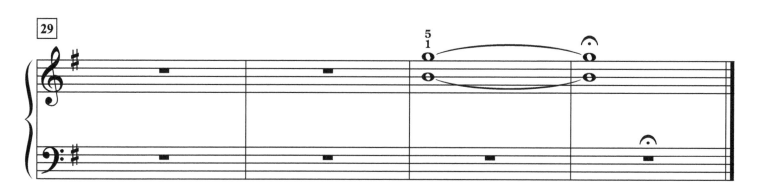

# The Pink Panther

## Secondo

By Henry Mancini
Arranged by Carol Matz

# The Pink Panther

## Primo

By Henry Mancini
Arranged by Carol Matz

**Secondo**

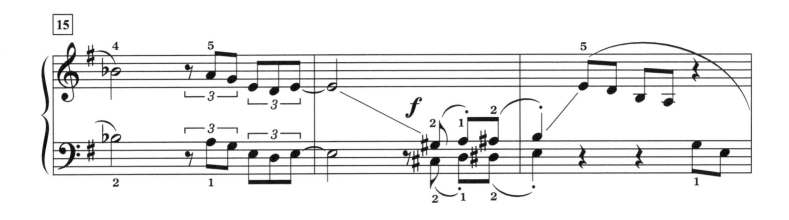

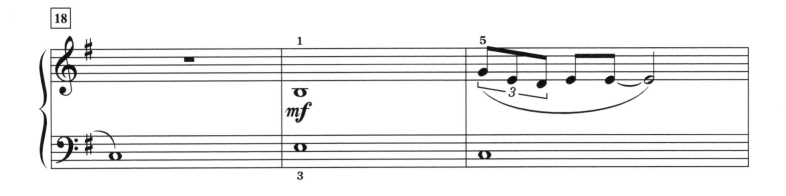

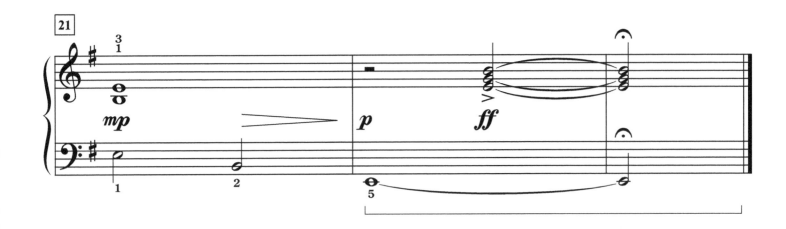

**Primo**

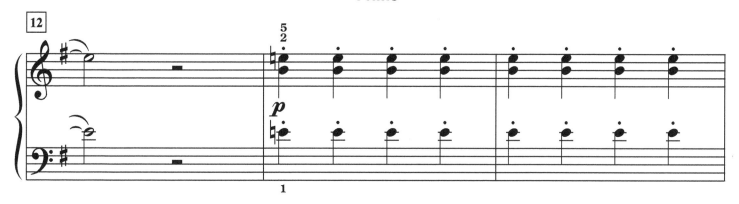

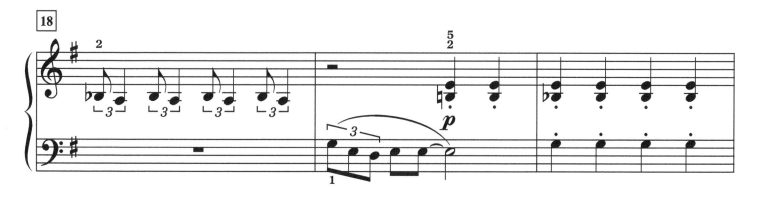

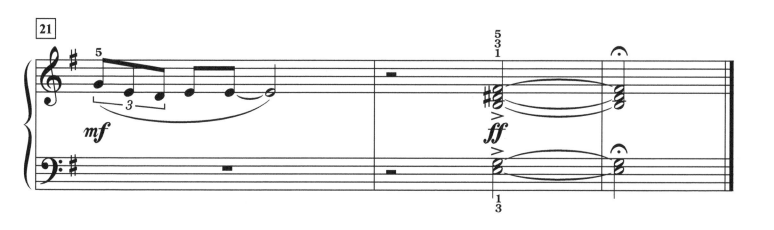